MW01622701

Surprising
NATURE

Other Books by Charles Mills

Pathfinder Honor series

The Bandit of Benson Park
Storm on Shadow Mountain
The Secret of Scarlett Cove
The Great Sleepy-Time Stew Rescue
Wings Over Oshkosh

Shadow Creek Ranch series

Escape to Shadow Creek Ranch
Whispers in the Wind
Danger in the Depths
Stranger in the Shadows
Out of the Blue

Eyes of the Crocodile
Refreshed Parables

Surprising Nature

Lessons from God's Creation

CHARLES MILLS *and* DORINDA KUEBLER MILLS

Nampa, Idaho | www.pacificpress.com

Cover design by Gerald Lee Monks
Cover design resources from Dorinda Kuebler Mills
Inside design by Aaron Troia
Interior photographs by Dorinda Kuebler Mills
Images on pp. 5–13 from GettyImages.com

Purchase additional copies of this book by calling toll-free 1-800-765-6955 or by visiting AdventistBookCenter.com.

ISBN 978-0-8163-6707-8

September 2020

Dedication

I dedicate the words of this book to my late father,
Robert C. Mills,
who taught me to see Jesus in everything.

Charles

For my nature girls,
niece Gianna Epperson and cousin Juliana Payne,
who find friends among the animals and share my love
for all of God's creatures.

Dorinda

Contents

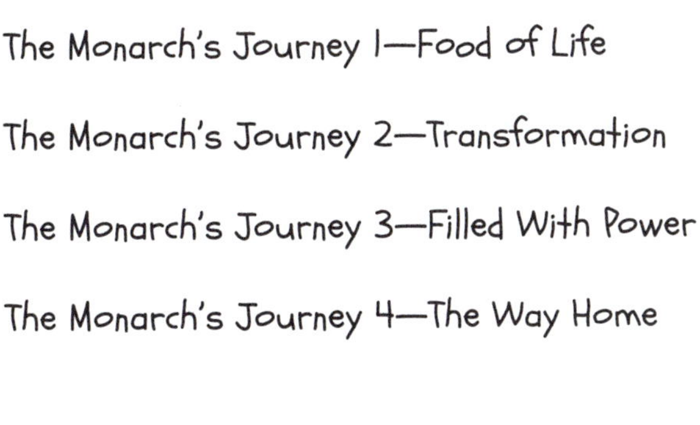

Welcome!

I remember it vividly. My dad and I were walking through a shaded wood in Syracuse, New York, listening to birds singing their spring songs. My binoculars were at the ready so I could catch a close-up view of whatever we found. I was fourteen years old at the time, and being with my father out in nature was my favorite activity. He knew so much about the critters that scurried among the shadows of the forest and the birds that filled the air with music.

Suddenly, a mother chickadee landed on a pine bough just above our heads. She was followed by two of her newly fledged young, both eager for whatever mom had to feed them. We watched spellbound as the little mealtime scene played out just inches away—no binoculars needed.

When the little family finally flew off in search of more goodies to eat, my dad whispered, "Charlie, that is how Jesus wants to take care of us. He wants to feed us with His words of love and protect us out here in this dangerous world."

Seeing God in nature comes naturally to me because of my dad. He uncovered powerful spiritual lessons in everything that happened, even the bad things. So, when my wife, Dorinda, began taking amazing pictures of God's creatures and sharing them with me, I kept hearing my dad's voice in the back of my mind telling me that there is something important to learn from this critter or that critter. I decided that young readers might enjoy learning those lessons too.

The result is this book. I like to believe that it was inspired by God—and my dad.

—*Charles*

I want to feel that I'm a part of nature, and I look forward to my outdoor adventures each day. I love watching and interacting with my critter friends. It's fun when a bird takes a seed from my hand or a butterfly or dragonfly lightly lands on my finger. I enjoy watching a praying mantis play for a few moments or coming nose to nose with a frog. Not long ago, during a walk in the woods, I spotted a very young fawn. She was standing next to a tree where her momma had left her to play. As I watched, she walked toward me. Those wobbly legs brought her right to my toes, and she began talking to me in her own special language. I looked into her sweet face and spoke softly. "Thank you for visiting me," I said. "I love you, little one."

Each spring I look forward to the arrival of a pair of Canada geese that come to our pond. I watch them as they search for food, swim, dive, and finally build a nest. Every day, for almost a month, I sit on a log close to the water's edge, keeping momma goose company as she incubates her eggs. She stays on the nest day and night. Dad comes and goes. But when hatch day arrives, he doesn't leave mom's side *at all!*

Mr. and Mrs. Goose allow me to sit nearby while their babies peck their way out of their shells. The goslings stick close to Mom as they tumble, play, and flap their tiny wings. They are oh so cute! By the next morning, the little ones are ready for their first swim, and off they go for other adventures far, far away. Blowing kisses as they leave, I wish them a safe and happy life. I hope you enjoy the memories I have captured with my camera. I also hope you will find fun outdoor adventures for yourself today and perhaps discover a new critter friend!

—Dorinda

Many Rooms

They build nests, raise young, protect their territory, and drift above the ground. No, they are not birds. They are fish!

Fish live in salt-water oceans, fresh-water rivers, and spring-fed mountain lakes. And like birds, their nests are sometimes built in sand, in caves, among rocks, or deep in a mound of dirt. Some fish even build their nests out of sticks, just like their feathered friends.

While many birds have big eyes so they can see clearly at night, fish depend on a special sense organ built right into their bodies that works like radar to help them move through dark or murky waters.

Jesus said, "There are many rooms in my Father's house" (John 14:2). He was talking about heaven. But it's the same here on earth. God's house of *nature* has "many rooms." The ocean is like a "room" filled with water and fish. The sky is a "room" filled with air, birds and bugs. We find mountain rooms, desert rooms, jungle rooms, and island rooms—all home to God's creatures. We may even live in one of those rooms.

So, when we look at a fish, we are simply peeking into one of God's many rooms—a hint of heaven where people of all kinds will live together forever.

"There are many rooms in my Father's house. . . . I am going there to prepare a place for you" (John 14:2).

This bluegill has something in common with birds and human beings.

The Big Thaw

Meet the frog. Frogs like to sit in the shallow waters of summer ponds and rivers and serenade each other. They catch bugs with their long, sticky tongues and hop here and there exploring their world. They can jump up high to capture flying insects and dive down deep under the ripples in search of food.

But it is what they do in the winter that is the real surprise. When cold winds blow and snow blankets the forest floor, some frogs sleep in trees, in underground burrows, under fallen logs, or even underwater. They are not only sleeping but are also frozen solid!

They don't eat. They don't hop. They don't sing. They just wait for spring to come, locked away in what scientists call "hibernation." They are not dead. They are just in a deep sleep.

Then, when the days grow longer and the sunlight warms the world, an amazing thing happens. Frozen frogs slowly thaw out! Before long, they blink their big eyes and look around. *Hey, now I can get back to eating and hopping and jumping*, they say to themselves in frog talk. *And I can sing too!* And they do.

Sometimes, sin captures us like a cold winter wind, and we stop doing what we know is right. Then Jesus' love thaws the cold in our hearts, and we can begin singing praises to Him once more. We might even hop and jump for joy!

Lord, even when I have trouble all around me, you will keep me alive (Psalm 138:7).

Gray tree frogs love to sing.

Giving Thanks

It can turn its head from front to back like an owl. Its eyes see the world in stereo just as we do. There is a special organ inside of it that can sense the silent vibrations that bats send out when hunting for food. And in many parts of the world, it's a much-loved pet.

Meet the praying mantis, a creature filled with surprises.

This beautiful animal lives in warm places and spends its time flying over meadows and streams searching for something to eat for about a year. It begins life as a tiny egg. While growing up, it can shed its skin like a snake up to ten times!

But most people don't think about this large insect's neck, eyes, special organ, or skin. They don't just notice its glassy wings, funny-shaped head, or jagged feet. They see something even more interesting. When not chasing another insect or flying among trees and bushes, the praying mantis sits quietly with its arms folded over its narrow chest. To many, the creature looks just like it is praying! That is how it got its name.

No one thinks the praying mantis is actually talking to God. But it can remind us that no matter how busy we are, how much fun we are having, or how worried we might be, we need to spend time with our hands folded in front of us, talking to the Creator of all things. God made praying mantises—and us. We can speak to Him every day and thank Him for all that He does for us.

Never stop praying. Give thanks whatever happens. That is what God wants for you in Christ Jesus (1 Thessalonians 5:17, 18).

A praying mantis looks like it is talking to God.

Future Beauty

The most surprising thing about this animal is its size. While most caterpillars are just an inch or so long, this one is huge! It can grow to be about six inches from nose to tail!

With all those mean-looking spines, horns, and bumps, you would think this creature would be dangerous, ready to give you a painful bite or sting! It even has a scary name: hickory horned devil. Would you want to touch anything with a name like that?

But you don't have to be afraid of this devil. There is no poison and no stingers in those spines and horns and bumps. They are there so birds and other animals who might want to eat the caterpillar will think, *Hey, that guy looks dangerous! I think I will go munch on some wild berries instead.*

This strange-looking, bumpy, spiny creature with horns doesn't stay like that for long. After about five weeks of eating plants and hanging out with the other animals of the fields and forest, something amazing happens. It burrows into the ground and stays there for a while. When it returns to the surface, those spines and horns and bumps are gone! It even has a new name—royal walnut moth. That is right! This large, strange-looking caterpillar changes into a big, beautiful moth with gray, green, and orange wings, ready to fly away.

When Jesus comes, He will change all of us strange-looking people who love Him into beautiful beings ready to fly away to heaven, where our beauty will last forever. Amazing!

We will be changed as quickly as an eye blinks. This will happen when the last trumpet sounds (1 Corinthians 15:52).

Hickory horned devils turn into beautiful moths.

Learning to Sing

How does a bird learn to sing? That is what scientists at Cornell University wanted to know. Does the mama or daddy bird teach it how to warble or chirp? Do other birds come over for a treetop voice lesson?

The answer is not only surprising, but it also teaches us something wonderful about God. The scientists discovered that each bird has its own special song already in its brain—and it doesn't even know it! So the young bird makes all kinds of chirps and warbles as it is growing up, but only when it sings a note that is part of its special song, does it feel a sudden happiness inside. *Hey, I like that note!* it might think to itself. *I need to sing that one again!*

When the bird finds other notes that bring it happiness, it starts arranging those notes into a melody or call that also makes it happy. That arrangement becomes its special song shared by all other birds who are just like it. That is why robins have their own special song, and sparrows have their own special song. Even crows have their very own special call!

God has put in us the information we need to live happy, healthy lives. When we do what God wants us to do, we feel happy. When we don't do what God wants us to do, we feel sad or afraid. He is teaching us the song of love, and we are the most joyful when we are singing it.

Sing and make music in your hearts to the Lord (Ephesians 5:19).

A blue-gray gnatcatcher sings its special song.

Sharing God's Love

Bees are busy insects. They fly here and there, buzzing around while looking for sweet nectar to drink from summer flowers. While they are sipping and enjoying the wonderful nectar, something surprising happens. Each flower has dusty pollen on it. *Pollen* is a special food that helps flowers grow tall and healthy. But flowers can't use their own pollen to do this. They need pollen from different flowers.

So along comes the thirsty bee, and while it's drinking nectar, pollen sticks to its legs, tummy, and wings. Then the bee buzzes to another flower, and all that pollen gets rubbed onto this new flower. More pollen gets on the bee from the new flower, and the bee moves on to yet another flower. Get the picture? Soon dozens of flowers are enjoying the pollen from dozens of other flowers, and everyone is happy—including the bee!

Missionaries are like bees. But they don't go from flower to flower. They go from person to person sharing the good news of God's love. Soon the whole world has heard about how Jesus died on the cross and wants to forgive our sins. We learn that Jesus can help everyone grow into kind, loving people.

What do missionaries get for all of their hard work? They enjoy the sweetness of Jesus' love filling their hearts with happiness. Everybody wins!

"Go everywhere in the world.
Tell the Good News to everyone"
(Mark 16:15).

Metallic-green bees share pollen like missionaries share God's love.

Here, There, and Everywhere

This little creature—three to four inches long—likes to move from place to place. It begins its life in a pond, lake, or stream, breathing oxygen from the water just like a fish.

Then two to five months later, it walks right up onto the shore, starts breathing air like a person, and changes color to a bright orange. For the next two to seven years, it wanders from place to place, looks for food, and finds hiding spots so other animals can't harm it.

Finally, it heads back to a pond, lake, or stream, changes color to a yellowish green, and lives up to twelve more years in the water. But this time it has to breathe air like a frog.

First, it breathes like a fish, then like a human, and then like a frog. It is so colorful and friendly that many boys and girls keep it as a pet.

Wherever it goes—wherever it lives—God provides not only air but also food and shelter. Underwater, out of water, in and out of water—it doesn't matter. God sees what it needs and helps it grow to live a long and healthy life.

Do not ever worry if you have to move to a new home, a new city, or even to a new country. God will be here, there, and everywhere, ready to be your Friend and care for you with loving kindness. What a wonderful God He is!

Nothing above us, nothing below us, or anything else in the whole world will ever be able to separate us from the love of God (Romans 8:38, 39).

The red-spotted newt lives on land—part of the time.

Storing for the Cold Winter

His name means "housekeeper" in the islands of Greece. In your backyard, you probably just call him a chipmunk. But it's what he does in the autumn of each year that may surprise you. He doesn't just eat nuts. He stores them—*lots* of them.

Winter can be hard on animals. Not only can cold, icy winds blow or snow pile up in deep drifts, but winter can also be a time when there is no food to eat. All the plants with seeds and nuts are either dead or sleeping away the winter. So what's a nut-loving critter to do?

Chipmunks know exactly what to do! As soon as leaves begin to turn from green to red, yellow, or orange, these little creatures get busy collecting nuts. Since their hands aren't very big—they can only carry one or two nuts at a time—they have found a great place to collect those precious nuts and seeds so they can carry them back to their den. They put them in their mouth!

Their cheeks can bulge out wide like balloons. This might make them look like they have a toothache, but they don't. They are just loaded down with seeds and nuts, which they carry to their underground or tree nests. Here they store enough food to see them through the coming winter.

Who taught them how to do this? The very same creator God who can teach us how to face anything the devil throws at us. Instead of storing nuts in a nest, we can store God's promises in our hearts, where they are ready to help us whenever winter winds blow.

I have taken your words to heart
so I would not sin against you (Psalm 119:11).

A chipmunk gets ready for cold winds to blow.

Old Skin, New Skin

It looks just like a dragonfly except for one surprising thing: there is no dragonfly in it! The animal has left its old skin behind and gone on to enjoy life in its brand-new skin. That is why you will find old skins here and there in a meadow, clinging to leaves or twigs, being blown by the wind through the grasses, or caught in some brambles.

As a dragonfly grows, its skin doesn't. For a time, that old skin helps protect the insides of the insect from the rain and sun. It gives the insect shape and lets us know that a dragonfly is a dragonfly. But unlike human beings, when the insides get too big for the outside, something surprising happens. A new skin begins to cover the dragonfly on the inside and soon everything is just too big for the old skin to hold. A tear appears, and the dragonfly—with its new and larger skin—simply crawls out of its old skin. Amazing!

Here is something else amazing: Someday you and I will do the same thing—sort of. When Jesus comes, the Bible says we will be changed in the blink of an eye. Our old, sinful selves will be gone, and new perfect selves will rise up to meet Jesus. We will leave all the old fear and old sorrow and old pain behind and begin new lives with Jesus in heaven. What a wonderful day that will be when we get our new skin, which we will proudly wear forever and ever!

We will be changed as quickly as an eye blinks. This will happen when the last trumpet sounds. . . . This body that will ruin must clothe itself with something that will never ruin (1 Corinthians 15:52, 53).

The old dragonfly
skin stays behind.

My, What Big Eyes!

You often hear them at night, somewhere in the darkness, calling out to each other. "Who, who are you? Who, who are *yoooooooou*?" From their lofty perch on a tree limb, they scan the darkness, looking for both food and enemies.

Scan the darkness? They can do that? Yes, thanks to a pair of amazingly large and very sensitive eyes. A barred owl's eyes are so big that they take up much of its face. Toss in a strong beak and some ears and there is no more room on its face.

Large eyes help the owl capture as much light as possible, even on a cloudy, moonless night. Add to that very sensitive ears, and you have a skillful night hunter.

Those big eyes are even more effective because barred owls can turn their heads 270 degrees. We can turn our heads up to 180 degrees. That means that barred owls can see more places without moving the lower part of their bodies and attracting unwanted attention.

Seeing and hearing is so important for all of God's creatures, including human beings. Sometimes, when we allow sin to enter our hearts and minds, we stop seeing and hearing the dangers around us. But God wants to heal us. He wants us to see and hear clearly. Then we can say, "Who, who am I? I'm God's child, and He loves me."

"But you [those who love Jesus] are blessed. You understand the things you see with your eyes. And you understand the things you hear with your ears" (Matthew 13:16).

A Fawn's Secret Weapon

Most everything in nature has a special smell. An elephant smells like an elephant. A lion smells like a lion. A bird smells like a bird. But there is one animal that doesn't smell like itself for a while—and that can save its life.

Animals that hunt and kill other animals for food depend on three important things to find their next meal: sight, sound, and smell. Into this dangerous world comes a baby white-tailed deer, better known as a "fawn." In order to survive, this little creature has to make sure that animals that would harm it don't notice him or her.

So the mother deer teaches her fawn to lie very still in the grass so it doesn't make any sounds. Nature has given the animal a beautiful spotted coat so it can blend in with the leaves and bushes around it, making it hard to see. But it's the third thing that is the most surprising. A newborn fawn does not have much odor or smell at all! He or she doesn't smell like a deer or an elephant or a lion. It doesn't smell like anything! So when a dangerous animal is nearby, it can't see it, hear it, or even smell it.

God loves to protect the creatures He created, including you and me. When we listen to our Creator's instructions in the Bible and follow His loving advice, it makes it harder and harder for the devil to harm us. Seems we have a secret weapon too!

The Lord will guard you from all dangers.
He will guard your life (Psalms 121:7).

Fawns are hard to hear, see, and smell.

Armor of God

This world is a dangerous place. If you are an animal, you need sharp fangs, fast legs, powerful wings, or the ability to jump high or dig low in order to escape danger. Turtles have none of those things. But they do stay close to home—really close.

Turtles carry their homes around with them. Their hard, protective shells give them a place to go *right now* when danger comes. They just tuck their legs, tails, and heads inside their shells and slam the doors shut! A dog may try to bite them, a bear may try to crush them, a snake may try to poison them, or a hawk may try to carry them away. But nothing works. They are safe and sound inside their homes, waiting for the danger to go away.

Have you ever wished you were a turtle when people were mean to you or hurt you by saying unkind things? Have you wished that you could just go inside your shell and be safe from their words and frowns? Well, you can! God has provided a shell for each one of us to use when Satan sniffs around wanting to do us harm. The Bible calls it—*armor*—which means "protection." Putting on this armor means we are allowing God to wrap His loving arms around us and protect us from sin while helping us chase away fear. The devil can't get us as long as we have our armor on.

Like the turtle, we are safe right where we are because God's protection goes wherever we go. All we have to do is ask for it and then follow the safety rules God has provided for us all.

Wear God's armor so that you can fight against the devil's evil tricks (Ephesians 6:11).

Eastern box turtles know about protection.

Blind and Hungry

Close your eyes. That is what the world looks like to a newborn bluebird. No light. No day or night. No trees or mountains or rivers. Everything is dark.

Then you hear the fluttering of wings, and suddenly, you know that you are not alone in your nest. Something is there with you. Something is adjusting the nesting material around you, making sure you are comfortable. Then that something gives you a tasty treat to eat!

Now the darkness doesn't seem so scary. Next, a soft, feathery body presses close to you, keeping you warm and chirping quietly in the stillness. Before long, you begin to hear other chirps and feel the movement of new brothers and sisters beside you.

Soon your eyes open, and you see the faces of your family for the first time. The darkness is gone. From then on, you live in a world of sounds and smells and interesting sights to see. You are growing up to be a beautiful bluebird. You will even discover you have your own special song to sing.

Living in this world of sin can be like being blind. It can sometimes be scary because you can't see anything good. Then you learn about Jesus. You learn that He cares for you and wants to keep you safe and happy. You learn that He has given you a loving mom or dad or grandmother or grandfather to care for you and teach you important things. When you learn about Jesus and His love and you invite Him into your heart, the darkness goes away.

"But one thing I do know. I was blind, and now I can see" (John 9:25).

A baby bluebird waits for dinner.

Tools for Protection

You see them on the beach, but they aren't working on their tans. They dig in the sand, but they aren't building a castle. And Atlantic ghost crabs have three surprising talents that help them stay alive.

First, Atlantic ghost crabs can make three different sounds. They use these sounds to "talk" with other crabs. They hit the sand with their claws. *Thump, thump, thump*. They rub their legs together. *Scratch, scratch, scratch*. And they make a bubbling sound with their mouths. *Bubble, bubble, bubble*. All of these sounds can warn other crabs of danger.

Their second talent is their rotating eyes. They can look forward, but they can also look to the left and to the right. Those amazing, club-shaped eyestalks can rotate their eyes all the way around so that they can even look backward. That is why it's pretty hard to sneak up on a crab.

Finally, they can change their color to better match their surroundings. When they are sitting on sand, they can become the sand's color. When they are sitting on rocks, they can blend in with the rocks. This helps them hide from their enemies.

God has given each of us ways to fight evil. First, we can talk to our friends and family and ask for guidance. Second, our heavenly Father can help us to see the dangers that surround us. Third, we can change our attitudes and become more and more like Jesus every day. These powerful tools help protect us from our meanest enemy—the devil!

The Lord will guard you as you come and go, both now and forever (Psalm 121:8).

Atlantic ghost crabs change colors to survive.

Hearing God's Voice

Many people are afraid of them because they look kind of creepy. They have fur, wiggly noses, pointy ears, and clawed feet. They often live in dark caves, and they can fly.

Little brown bats are what scientists call *mammals*. That means their blood is warm, they have hair or fur, make milk to feed their young, and most give birth to live babies. We are mammals, too, so bats are like us—only a lot smaller. Oh, but we can't fly.

But what is most surprising about bats is that they can fly around in total darkness. They have perfectly good eyes to see when there is light. But how do they fly around in caves or at night when there is no light? How do they keep from running into things or each other? With sound.

Bats make very high-pitched squeaks. But that is not what helps them the most. Those squeaks travel out of their mouths, hit an object like a cave wall or another bat, and then the sound bounces back to them. They are able to hear the squeaks' returning echo and determine if an object is in their way. They can figure out how close an object is and what shape it is by the returning sounds. Humans have radar that can do that for us. We also have God to help us.

The next time you see a bat flying around or hanging in a cave, think about how our prayers go from us to God. He talks to us, warning us of dangers and telling us what we need to do to avoid sin and the pain it can bring. Bats always listen, so should we.

If you go the wrong way—to the right or to the left—you will hear a voice behind you. It will say, "This is the right way. You should go this way" (Isaiah 30:21).

Little brown bats
are always listening.

The Language of Smell

If we want to tell someone something, we talk. "How are you?" we say. "You look nice in your new hat." If a bird wants to say something to another bird, it sings or chatters. *Tweet, tweet, tweet. Chatter, chatter, chatter.* If a mink wants to say something, it makes a smell!

Mink are beautiful animals with thick, soft, dark fur. The fur has a layer of oil on it, so mink can swim across a pond, lake, or stream and not get wet. The water just runs right off, like on a duck with its oily feathers. The mink has thin skin growing between its toes, so it can quickly swim away from danger just like a duck.

But it is the mink's nose that is the most surprising part of its body. With it, it can smell dangerous animals coming, know if it is entering the territory of another mink that may not be too happy to see it, or find a mate. We might say to someone we meet, "I *see* you." A mink—if it could talk—would say to a friend or family member, "I *smell* you." Mink (and you) can smell even with eyes closed and ears covered, so they are always alert to danger.

God has given all animals, including people, the ability to identify danger. We may recognize it by sight; by sound; or even, like a mink, by smell. We need to use all of our senses to keep one step ahead of the devil. When we recognize the sight, sound, or smell of evil, we can do like the mink does—run away fast!

"The Lord's loved ones will lie down in safety. The Lord protects them all day long. The ones the Lord loves rest with him" (Deuteronomy 33:12).

Mink communicate with their noses.

Alphabet of Sound

People who speak English use twenty-six different letters—everything from A to Z—to talk with each other. We combine those twenty-six letters to make the words that we read or speak. But that is nothing compared to raccoons!

When raccoons talk to each other, they use sounds. How many sounds? *Two hundred!* They are combining two hundred sounds to make their "words." Can you even imagine what it would be like to learn how to talk in raccoon?

These surprising creatures with their black masks are great tree climbers. They can also scamper up buildings; walls; and, if you let them—*you*! All they are looking for is food. Their little paws are very much like your hands. They can open doors, unscrew jars, pop open bottles, and lift gate latches with ease.

Have you ever wondered what the language of heaven will be like? Maybe it will be like "raccoon," with lots of kind and loving sounds as well as words. Don't worry. We will learn heaven's language very quickly. How? Maybe the animals will teach us using their special noises. We might learn how to say hello in bird, lion, or hippopotamus. Sounds like fun, doesn't it? But for now, just know that when you speak to God, He hears and understands every word—even if you happen to be a raccoon.

Lord, every morning you hear my voice. Every morning, I tell you what I need. And I wait for your answer (Psalm 5:3).

Raccoons talk
in sounds—lots
of sounds.

Seeds of Kindness

Every fall there is a creature that gets especially busy. It scampers here and there gathering nuts—the ones still in trees and those that have fallen to the ground. Many of those nuts get stored in the creature's nest high in the trees. Many others—hundreds of them—get buried in the ground.

That creature is the squirrel, a hardworking rodent with a bushy tail and front teeth that never stop growing.

What is most amazing about this animal is that it doesn't forget where it puts those nuts—any of them! It can eat them or dig them up anytime it wants. Sometimes winter isn't long or harsh, and those buried nuts never get unburied. So what do they do? They grow up and become trees where squirrels can build more nests.

What a beautiful picture of how God cares for His creatures—including us. We can go about planting seeds of kindness in people's minds. We can smile at them, help them when they are in trouble, and say comforting words when they feel sad. Then, one day, we might need help or kindness, and that seed we planted in someone else might grow into an act of kindness for us! They help us. They smile at us. They say comforting words when we are sad.

"Be like the squirrel," God's nature tells us. "You never know when you might need a forest."

How many seeds of kindness will you plant this week?

A person harvests only what he plants (Galatians 6:7).

What squirrels
don't eat may
become a forest.

My Home Is Your Home

Question: How do you know that a muskrat has been in your yard?

Answer: If you see paw prints that have both four toes (small front paws) and five toes (larger back paws). And between them, you see a long line in the soil created by a skinny tail. You might also see droppings on top of stumps, logs, and rocks.

These small, furry animals are common in North America. They live for about three years in the wild, and they spend their time on land and in the water.

But the most surprising thing about muskrats is that certain birds depend on them for nesting spots. How? Muskrats level out places on the ground by eating the plants that grow there. They also build strong lodges (above-ground dens) in swampy areas. This provides several kinds of birds safe, dry places to build their nests.

This sharing of spaces makes the muskrat an important part of nature. One animal helps to provide for another.

God wants us to learn from the muskrat. He wants us to help others in everything we do. He wants us to share our talents, our hard work, and our concern for safety with those around us.

So if someone calls you a "muskrat," say, "Thank you. I'm proud to be like that beautiful creature that helps others." Then go out and help others.

Open your homes to each other, without complaining. . . . Use your gifts to serve each other (1 Peter 4:9, 10).

Muskrats love
to share.

Big Eyes Looking at You!

It lives in wooded areas and tries its best to avoid attention. But sometimes it trips on a twig or lands crooked after a short flight and ends up on its back. That is a dangerous place to be! Not to worry. It simply snaps a part of its body, and this action propels it up into the air where it spins around and, hopefully, lands right side up. It's also a quick way to escape a predator.

The sound it makes when it performs this flip gives the creature its name—eastern eyed *click* beetle. But it has another surprising talent. This bug has a secret weapon to prevent another animal from trying to catch and eat it—big eyes! Except, its eyes are not truly big. They just *look* big.

The click beetle's eyes are actually small. But God has given this insect thick, white rings that surround each "eye." Predators see those big "eyes" and say to themselves, "Whoa. That must be a dangerous insect. Look at those huge eyes! I'm not bothering that critter, no sir!"

The ability to move fast and the appearance of huge eyes give the click beetle a fighting chance to survive.

God offers us the same tools. He can help us run away from temptation and make us look very strong against the devil. With Jesus living in our hearts, Satan doesn't see a little kid. He sees a powerful God looking back at him. "I'm not bothering that child," he says. *Click!*

"But those who listen to me will live in safety. They will be safe, without fear of being hurt" (Proverbs 1:33).

Eastern eyed click beetles look mean, but they aren't.

Hiding in Plain Sight

You have probably walked by one many times. One may have watched you enjoy a picnic lunch in the park, but you never knew it was there. Why? Because it looked like part of a bush.

Walking sticks got their name because they look like sticks that can walk. This lets them hide in plain sight, perfectly blending into their surroundings. They are usually brown, black, or green. Some have markings that look like lichen (moss) so they can sit on a rock without being seen. They will rock back and forth exactly like a stick that is blowing in the wind. Some will even play dead if they are threatened. No animal wants to eat a dead stick!

Walking sticks hide in plain sight.

Here is a surprising fact. If a predator does grab on to them and yanks off an arm or leg, the walking stick can grow a new one.

In order to survive in this sinful world, you and I have to learn how to hide in plain sight too. If we ask God, He will cover us with love and kindness. That helps us treat others with respect. We will help others instead of running away. We will forgive when someone is mean to us. We will even allow God to create a new heart in us when our old one is broken by sadness or anger. So when people look at us, they don't see evil. They see Jesus.

He will protect you like a bird spreading its wings over its young. His truth will be like your armor and shield (Psalm 91:4).

Split Personality

Is it a bird or a bug? Many people who see the amazing hummingbird moth for the first time may be a little confused. It buzzes, it hovers, and it flits from flower to flower like a hummingbird. But if you look closely, you will discover that it has a long, flexible, straw-like tongue instead of a stiff beak. Its wings—if you can catch them at rest—are clear in the middle. It is definitely a moth.

The hummingbird moth buzzes and hums just like a hummingbird, but there is not one feather in sight. And while both bird and bug are fun to watch, they are certainly not the same creature. The moth spends part of its life cycle as a caterpillar. The bird goes straight from egg to bird.

What is surprising about the moth is that it can remind us about what it is like to live with Jesus in our hearts. We are human, and yet we are children of God. We can have smiles on our faces (like God), even when we are going through a difficult situation (like humans). We sometimes make mistakes and sin (human), but we know that we are forgiven (God). People can look at us and say, "Now there is a child of God," even when we are struggling as a human being.

The hummingbird moth reminds us of the hummingbird by the way it looks and acts. We can remind people of God the very same way.

"You should be a light for other people. Live so that they will see the good things you do. Live so that they will praise your Father in heaven" (Matthew 5:16).

The hummingbird moth is like two critters in one.

Born Ready

It takes them up to two days to escape from their eggs. To earn their freedom, baby Canada geese (goslings) peck at their shells with a special "egg tooth" found at the end of their bills. Once free from their eggs, they are walking, swimming, and feeding within twenty-four hours. And before long, they are diving thirty to forty feet underwater looking for food.

They need to eat a lot of strength-building plant foods because they must be ready to do battle with foxes, eagles, owls, and falcons right from the start. These predators don't think of them as cute, feathery friends but as a meal!

Between eight and twelve weeks after hatching, goslings learn to fly. A few short weeks later, they fly south—sometimes as far as Mexico. Yes, they have to learn how to survive *fast*!

But they have help. Mom and Dad stay nearby. Goslings learn by watching and copying their parents. They practice skills that will help protect them for many years.

God watches over His creation with tender love, teaching anyone who is willing to learn how to survive the dangers hiding all around. He works through Moms and Dads, other relatives, faithful friends, school teachers, and even kind neighbors. They can reveal God's love in many ways, providing instruction for learning how to live a safe and happy life.

The Lord says, "I will make you wise. I will show you where to go. I will guide you and watch over you" (Psalm 32:8).

Baby Canada geese, "goslings," learn fast.

When Blue Jays Forget

It's fall, and blue jays begin to act like squirrels. They find food and bury it. And while they are busy putting snacks in the ground, something amazing is happening to their brains.

One part of the bird's brain grows larger. It's the part where memories are stored (the hippocampal region). In this newly developed area of the brain, the bird keeps track of where it put all of those delicious winter treats. Throughout the cold months, the bird can easily find those buried morsels and enjoy a quick, tasty meal.

When spring arrives, and bugs (its usual food) reappear in abundance, that part of the bird's brain shrinks, and he forgets where he buried the rest of the nuts and seeds. Without being eaten, the nuts and seeds begin to grow. Soon a new forest appears right out of the ground.

Have you ever wondered how you will act when temptation comes? Have you ever worried whether you will know enough to make good decisions? Well, we need to remember that we serve a God who is able to actually grow our brains so that we can recall what we need to remember when we need to remember it. He gives us knowledge when we need it most.

So don't be afraid of the future. God is preparing us now to face whatever is coming. The good news is that when we get to heaven, we won't remember the hard, sad times. He will help us forget.

You know when I sit down and when I get up.
You know my thoughts before I think them (Psalm 139:2).

Surprising facts
about a noisy
neighbor.

Breaking Point

Have you ever been tempted to do something mean or selfish? Have you ever hurt someone when you were angry? We all struggle with sin and that is why we need to meet the eastern fence lizard. It can teach us a surprising lesson.

Lizards have a series of bones that run down their back and the length of their tail. In their tail, God has created several weak points in the bones. When the lizard is attacked by a predator or something grabs its tail, the bones separate at one of those weak points and the tail comes right off! It wiggles and squirms as if it is still attached. The animal that is attacking the lizard gets so focused by the wiggling tail that the lizard can run away to safety.

Eastern fence lizards defend themselves.

A partial new tail will eventually grow back, but for a while, the lizard looks shorter than before. It may also have learned a valuable lesson about where *not* to go when looking for food.

When someone is mean to us or hurts us, we need to do what the lizard does. We need to let go of the problem—even if that means we will be sad for a while. We need to forgive and forget. But don't worry, God will help us grow our happiness back, and we will be as good as new. Like the eastern fence lizard, we will be our old selves again with a brand-new tail!

Maybe Jesus was thinking about the lizard when He gave His followers the advice found in Matthew 18:9.

"If your eye causes you to sin, take it out and throw it away. It is better for you to have only one eye but have life forever" (Matthew 18:9).

Toxic Skin

You can find them in the forest, under leaves, in little rain-filled ponds, and along streams. Look for them after a summer shower, but don't bother searching for them in the winter time. They are sleeping underground.

Spotted salamanders can live up to twenty years and lay hundreds of eggs each year. Many of them don't survive after hatching, but while they are still in their eggs, they and their many, many brothers and sisters are protected by a white, milky mass.

But it is the adult salamander that enjoys something unique. On its back and tail are glands just below the skin that, when the animal is threatened, pump out a toxic, sticky substance that tastes terrible to the creatures who might try to eat them. Yuck! Creatures trying to eat a salamander often spit them out.

Did you know that God offers to make us "taste terrible" to those who would do us harm? Like the spotted salamander, we have enemies who want to do mean things to us such as make fun of us, embarrass us, or even hurt us if they can. But long ago, God created a protection for us to use. It's called "love." People who don't love God don't want to be around us. They would rather follow Satan and enjoy the sweetness of sin for a while. When we surround ourselves with God's love, we can live joyfully even in this dangerous world.

The Lord will guard you from all dangers. He will guard your life (Psalms 121:7).

Spotted salamanders don't taste good to predators.

I See You

Do you ever wish you had eyes in the back of your head? Think how good you would be at sports! Well, there is a spider that would make a great second baseman except for the fact that it is—well—a spider. It can see things in very surprising ways.

Wolf spiders got their name because they don't spin webs to catch a meal. They chase down their prey and pounce on it—like wolves. What helps them chase and pounce? Eight eyes!

They have two large eyes sitting on the top of their heads, two more peering out the front, and a row of four smaller eyes just above their mouths.

Why would a little creature need so many eyes? Because they not only have to *find* prey, but they also *are* prey. There are plenty of animals who would love to have them over for dinner, literally.

All of those eyes can help them see when a bird or some other critter is creeping up on them. They can say, "I *see* you!" and then hop, skip, or jump away to live another day.

We can think of God as our extra set of eyes. He willingly warns us when sin is trying to creep up on us. He says, "Run away!" by making us feel uncomfortable and afraid of things that can hurt us. It is like having eyes in the back of our heads.

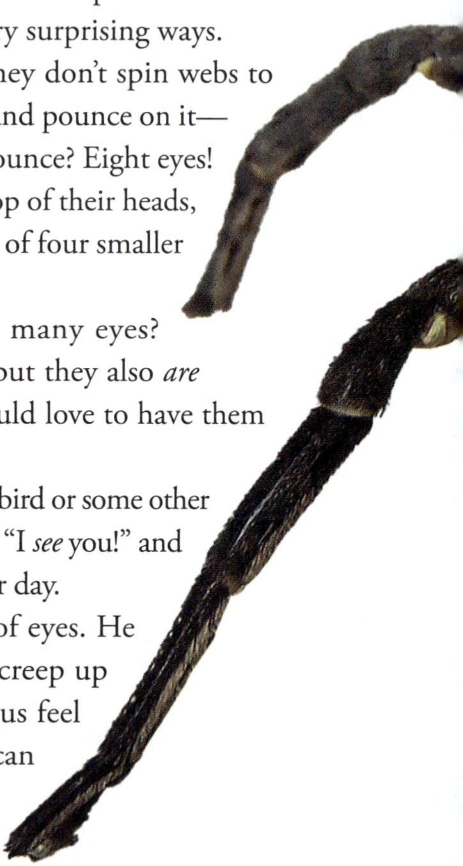

The Lord is my light and the one who saves me (Psalm 27:1).

A wolf spider keeps an eye on you—all eight of them.

Different but Not Different

When you see one, you might gasp. Yes, it may have the same beautiful eyes, nose, and hooves as other deer, but large sections of its fur are white instead of brown.

They are called "piebald" deer and they are not common. That is a good thing because piebald deer can also suffer from an arching spine, a shortened lower jaw, deformed legs, a chew-disturbing overbite, bowed nose, and some very crippling problems inside their bodies.

But here is the thing. Some piebald deer can live long lives. They can have babies and care for them. They run and play—sometimes with difficulty—with the other deer in the herd. God freely sends the rain to grow the plants that they eat, gives them instincts that will help protect them from predators, and provides a warm coat of winter fur to help when cold winds blow.

To God, piebald deer are the same as the other animals, even though they are different. He loves all of His creatures the same, no matter how they look or what health challenges they face.

That is how *we* should love people. They may be different, but our job is to love and protect them, just as God loves and protects us. After all, compared to the angels, we probably look pretty strange! We are sinful. We are sick. But we are loved.

Christ died for us while we were still sinners. In this way God shows his great love for us (Romans 5:8).

This white-tailed deer stands out in the herd.

Superpower

Sniff, sniff, sniff. Dogs do that a lot. *Sniff, sniff, sniff.* That is because their noses are their superpower. They can breathe in and out at the same time so they don't lose a scent. And you know how our human eyes give us a three-dimensional view of the world, revealing not only what an object is but how far away it happens to be? Well, a dog's nose can smell with each nostril separately so they know not only what the smelly object is but also where it is.

Smelly things, such as people and animals, leave scents behind even after they have left the area. While you and I usually can't smell an object after its odor has faded, dogs can smell an object long after what

A dog's nose is its superpower.

made it has vanished from view. That is why tracking dogs can sniff the ground and follow a person or animal for miles even though what they are tracking has not been nearby for hours—sometimes even days. Many a lost person has been very thankful for that particular dog superpower.

Have you ever wondered why a dog's nose is wet? That wetness—a mixture of saliva (dog spit) and mucus (something the dog makes in its nose to keep it moist)—captures scent particles floating in the air. Then their brain can take its time to figure out what made them.

The Creator God gives all of His creatures superpowers. For the dog, it goes *sniff, sniff, sniff.* For us humans, it can go love, love, love. Both superpowers can save people.

God . . . gives life to everyone who walks on the earth (Isaiah 42:5).

Keeping Cool

Pretend you are playing outside on a hot summer day and you get overheated. What do you do? You head for a shady spot or run inside for a cool drink of water. Blue dasher dragonflies like shade too. But if no shade is available, they do something surprising.

Since sunlight warms whatever it shines on, blue dashers point the end of their bodies at the sun. This limits the amount of sun exposure to their bodies. They can also tilt their wings forward and down. This helps keep even more sun off their bodies. The result is relief from the heat.

Blues also stand on their feet with their abdomens straight up in the air and their wings and heads down while guarding their territories or when doing battle with other males who want to take away their partners. Even during battle, blue dashers keep their cool.

Here is another advantage of standing with abdomen straight up and wings and head down. Dragonflies can absorb moisture through their skin. So on cool, foggy mornings, they can treat themselves to a nice drink without going anywhere. They stay safe on their twig or bush and satisfy their thirst at the same time. Very clever!

If God can teach blue dashers to keep their cool, He can certainly teach you and me the same thing. He will show us how to face evil and keep our love for others no matter how and where we need to stand up for Him.

Love . . . does not become angry easily
(1 Corinthians 13:5).

Humans have
air conditioners.
Blue dashers
point at the sun.

Knock on Wood

You can hear them for miles—woodpeckers pecking on wood. They "drum" to catch the attention of mates and to drill holes in trees to find delicious bugs to eat. Sometimes they even drill holes in wooden houses! But if you and I were to hit our heads against a piece of wood like that, we would knock ourselves silly or do some serious damage to our noses. What do woodpeckers have that we don't?

First, they know how to stand so that their large neck muscles, instead of their smaller face muscles, absorb the shock. While our bones are thick and hard, theirs are spongy—like a bicycle helmet. That makes them stretchy. Their long tongue wraps around their skull instead of starting in their throats. Our top and bottom lips are about the same size, but the woodpecker's upper beak is much thicker and stronger than its lower beak. That makes it better for knocking on wood.

Their brains are long and narrow instead of fat and round like ours. And while our brains are surrounded by liquid, bird brains are not. There is very little fluid to slosh around and allow their brains to get out of place while they drill into trees.

In other words, God gave woodpeckers the tools to do all the things that they need to do. If God wants us to do something—like love and care for people—we can be sure that He has given us the built-in tools we need too. Woodpeckers peck on wood. We share God's love.

The Lord your God will make you successful in everything you do (Deuteronomy 30:9).

This downy woodpecker can peck hard without scrambling its brain.

Beat the Drum Loudly

They are some of the loudest insects on earth. When they "sing" (make a buzz-like sound), they can be heard for great distances. When a bunch of them "sing" together, it makes you want to cover your ears and run away. But that is the point.

Cicadas have a built-in musical drum in their body. The muscles they use to create their unique sounds are called "tymbals." They create their sound by making those muscles get smaller and then larger very quickly. This makes a *click*. Their abdomen is mostly hollow, so that clicking sound is amplified, just as when you beat on a drum.

Why all the noise? First, they want to attract a mate, so they sit in a tree and announce: "Here I am!" They can also change their sound to let everyone know that there is danger nearby.

And guess what doesn't like very loud sounds? Birds. And Birds eat cicadas. So to protect themselves from being a meal, they drum out their sound with great enthusiasm. Birds can't stand the noise, and they leave the cicadas alone. Mission accomplished!

Ever wish you had a sound that would help protect you from the devil? Well, you do! When you speak the name of Jesus—when you sing praises or whisper prayers to Him—something amazing happens. Jesus hears and answers. And the devil? He runs away.

But I will call to God for help.
And the Lord will save me.
Morning, noon and night I am troubled and upset.
But he will listen to me (Psalm 55:16, 17).

Cicadas "sing" for protection.

Slow and Steady

How long does it take you to run across your front yard? Fifteen seconds? Ten seconds? Unless you live on a farm, your front yard probably isn't very big.

If you were a snail, you would need to pack a lunch for the same trip. The speediest of all snails only moves around fifty yards an *hour!* And they are mostly muscle!

A snail's body is like a foot with a head attached on one end. Unlike some creatures, snails don't shed their shells as they grow. Their shells grow right along with them.

Snails eat by both chewing food and soaking up nutrients through their amazing muscle/foot. Their eyes are perched on the end of wiggly stems that stick out of their face.

But here is the thing. Everything works together perfectly. Their foot, their face, their eyes, their shell—all of these body parts are necessary for a snail to be a successful, living and breathing snail.

It's the same with you and me. Our body parts—our arms, legs, faces, and ears—are part of what make us who we are. Keep in mind that God made each of us for a purpose—to love and care for others, some of whom don't look anything like us. But that is OK. It doesn't matter that we look different. Love doesn't notice the differences.

So the next time you see a snail, just say to it, "Hey snail, I understand what it's like to be you. God made me just like He wants me to be too."

I praise you because you made me in an amazing and wonderful way (Psalm 139:14).

A snail is in no hurry,
even when it is in a hurry.

Prepared

It always comes sooner or later—the winds, the cold, the snow. Groundhogs know this, and they begin a yearly autumn ritual that will save their lives.

First, you need to know that the word *groundhog* is their common name. Scientists called them *monax* which means "solitary." And that means "I like being alone, thank you very much." And being alone is what groundhogs do best. They live in underground burrows and spend their time searching for plants to eat—alone. Even their young are kicked out of the burrow when they are just two months old. No, these are not social animals. Other than enjoying group protection, they are very happy to be totally alone.

When groundhogs sense the approach of winter, they eat an extra helping of everything. All that food is stored as body fat inside them. Then, as winter grips the land above their underground burrows, they go to sleep (hibernate) and let their bodies provide nourishment by using all that stored fat. In other words, they stay alive with the food they ate before they needed it.

We are not groundhogs, but God wants us to do the very same thing with the Bible. He wants us to enjoy extra helpings of His words of instruction and comfort so that when we need it, we will have nourishment waiting to comfort and save us.

I have taken your words to heart
so I would not sin against you (Psalm 119:11).

Groundhogs store up food for winter in a surprising place.

Sweet Service

They must gather nectar (the liquid made by flowers) from two million plants to make one pound of something humans love to eat. To do this, they have to fly about ninety thousand miles. That is equal to flying three times around the earth!

But here is the thing. Each animal produces only around one-twelfth of a teaspoon of this special food, and they spend their lifetime doing it. It takes a lot of work to make a little bit of this food. But do they complain? Nope! They just buzz off to find more nectar for their hive.

What amazing creature is this? The tiny, very busy honey bee. What do they make? Honey. This bee-created gift is a kid favorite and a frequent topping on breakfast cereals.

Honey is also used to ease sore throats and coughs. Some scientists are doing studies to discover what other healing benefits honey may have.

Did you know that *you* can make something sweet for this world too? It might not be a cereal topping, but your sweet, kind words can bring comfort to a sad heart. Your acts of kindness can ease the soreness of sin and heal the damage of wrong choices. Love is sweet. Share it often.

Pleasant words are like a honeycomb.
They make a person happy and healthy (Proverbs 16:24).

Honey bees create
a sweet surprise.

Built-in Protections

Ever wonder why it's so hard to sneak up on a rabbit? The answer sits on top and on each side of its head.

While an owl can turn its head around and look behind him while sitting on a perch, a rabbit can check out what is going on without moving an inch. Rabbits' eyes can see almost 360 degrees—that is every direction *at once*. Not only that, their tall, furry ears can rotate forward and backward so they can hear the slightest sound no matter where it is coming from.

Rabbits have one more feature to keep them safe: long, powerful legs. They can be hopping at full speed almost instantly, leaving a fox, wolf, or cat wondering, *Hey, where did my meal go?* Some rabbits can cover ten feet with each hop. That is fast!

Can you do what rabbits can do? Of course not. You are not a rabbit. But you serve the God who *made* rabbits, and He can see and hear danger immediately. He can warn you with feelings of doubt and fear whenever Satan tries to sneak up on you. When Satan tries to trick you, God can help you run away fast—like a rabbit.

I go to bed and sleep in peace.
Lord, only you keep me safe (Psalm 4:8).

Rabbits have three built-in protectors.

Little Stinker

You may have seen them on some blossoms and grasses in your backyard. You have probably admired their bright-red bodies and little black spots. You may have asked yourself, "Are these pretty little bugs helpful or harmful to my mom's or dad's garden?" The answer is *helpful*. They eat bugs that eat plants—including the vegetable plants growing in neat rows in your family garden. Yes, ladybugs are a gardener's best friend.

What you may not know (because you don't eat ladybugs) is that they pump out some sort of yellow liquid from their body whenever a predator grabs them. That sticky, yellow liquid smells *terrible* to the predator, and they stop their attack immediately. Ladybugs also taste bad. Not only that, even their color will scare away predators. Apparently, predators don't like red with black spots.

Would you like to look and smell bad to Satan? You can! You can fill your heart with Jesus' love, which makes you look friendly and peaceful. The devil hates friendly and peaceful people. You can also share God's love with others. The Bible says that the knowledge of God's love is like a sweet-smelling perfume. So go ahead, fill the world with love. The devil hates that. He would rather have you look and smell just like him.

God uses us to spread his knowledge everywhere like a sweet-smelling perfume (2 Corinthians 2:14).

Ladybugs defend themselves by stinking.

Sing Louder

In a quiet meadow or on a mountainside among towering trees, grasshoppers sing softly to each other. They call out for mates in gentle tones and announce their territories with the soothing songs they create by rubbing their legs against their wings. But in the city, their songs change dramatically.

Scientists are discovering something surprising about grasshoppers. When the noise level around them goes up, such as when traffic is roaring, air conditioners are humming, or machines are running, grasshoppers turn up the volume of their singing. Like whales, birds, and frogs, these little insects, over time, leave their inside voices behind and announce their presence with decidedly louder outside voices. They want to be heard!

Sometimes Satan wants to drown out your soft praises to God. He wants to silence your prayers. So he pumps up the noise of sin in your life.

What should you do? Follow the grasshopper's lead and pray, sing, and praise louder. Be joyful louder. Tell God that you love Him louder. And then announce to the noisy world, "God loves you!" This is no time to be quiet. It's time to shout what you believe to others. Your friends, family, and even strangers will hear you.

Let the sea and everything in it shout.
Let the fields and everything in them show
their joy (1 Chronicles 16:32).

Grasshoppers are finding a way to be heard.

Weapon of Choice

Some animals fight. Some run away from danger. Skunks have a unique way of telling a dangerous predator, "Don't mess with me!" And it is not its nasty-smelling spray. It is its stripes!

Scientists discovered that many animals have markings that draw attention to their best and most efficient weapon. Badgers have stripes pointing to sharp teeth. Skunks have stripes that point to its sprayer. It is like they are saying, "Mess with me and you will get a load of *this*!" If the predator takes the hint and leaves, skunks don't have to use their most powerful weapon and then be vulnerable for a time while their bodies makes more stinky stuff.

These critters also have another weapon—dancing. They will move through a series of motions like stomping the ground, slapping their tails against nearby objects, and even doing a handstand or two. Predators think, *There is something wrong with this animal!* and they leave. Of course, if all else fails, there is always the trusty sprayer.

Skunks have learned that it is better to warn off an attacker than to actually fight to the death. They know that violence isn't the answer to any situation, and they do what they can to keep things from getting out of control. If your enemy walks away from a fight, you have won the battle.

That is an important lesson for all of us to learn. Nonviolence should be our weapon of choice.

A person who quickly gets angry causes trouble. But a person who controls his temper stops a quarrel (Proverbs 15:18).

The skunk's
stripes help keep
it out of fights.

The Need for Speed

Everything about this bird is an "est." It's the small*est*, fast*est*, light*est* bird in the air. It even makes the tini*est* eggs in the tini*est* bird's nest. Some insist that it's the pretti*est* too.

Hummingbirds don't hum. The sound people hear is their wings moving through the air at such a high speed that they create a "humming" sound that changes pitch (high and low) as these birds maneuver around flowers, sipping nectar through their long tongues and bills.

Even hummingbirds' hearts are fast, beating up to 1,200 times per minute when they are flying. A healthy human heart might reach around 170 beats per minute while a person is running hard. Those hummingbird wings move so fast that they look like a blur, reaching 70 beats (up and down) per *second* while flying and 200 beats per second while diving. Try that with *your* arms.

These birds can fly eighteen to twenty hours without stopping during migration over the Gulf of Mexico. At an average speed of thirty miles per hour, that is up to six hundred miles between rest stops. Can you do that?

So don't ever think that because you are short, tall, large, skinny, or look different than other people that you are limited. There may even be mean people who make fun of you because you are not like them. Relax! God has special abilities built into you that He wants you to use to love others—even the mean ones. You can start by being the kind*est* person around.

I can do all things through Christ because he gives me strength (Philippians 4:13).

Ruby-throated hummingbirds drink in a hurry.

Play to Survive

It looks like fun. If you hang out near a river otter den, usually located at the very edge of a body of water, you will see a lot activity. While the older otters are busy keeping house and finding food for the family, the young otters are often running, sliding, jumping, tackling, chasing, pouncing, splashing, swimming, diving, bumping, and wrestling. Are they playing games? Sort of. But something else is going on—something important. Those young otters are learning how to stay alive in a dangerous world.

Their quick movements are keeping them fit and strong. Their leaps and dives are teaching them how to get away from animals that want

River otters learn how to survive by playing games.

to harm them. They are learning teamwork, how to protect each other, and how to escape when something is chasing them through the woods or waters. At the end of the day, when they lay down to rest or sleep, they are simply taking a break from the training necessary to survive in the wild.

You can take a lesson from river otters. When you play your favorite games, when you interact in a fun way with other people, when you compete in a race or try to win a contest, you have a great opportunity to practice honesty, fairness, and playing by the rules. Every game can be a learning experience. Then, when you rest, you can know that you have trained well too.

Train a child how to live the right way. Then even when he is old, he will still live that way (Proverbs 22:6).

The Monarch's Journey 1

Food of Life

It begins life as a tiny egg stuck to the bottom of a milkweed leaf. Before it becomes a monarch butterfly, the monarch caterpillar—which hatches from that tiny egg—requires a very specific plant for food so it can grow strong and healthy. Yes, you guessed it—milkweed. There are several types of milkweed plants, and the monarch loves them all.

As the caterpillar grows, it sheds its old skin. This happens several times. The "cat," as some call it, lives on the milkweed, sleeps on the milkweed, and eats the milkweed leaves. It is home sweet home for the monarch caterpillar.

Are we like that little creature? In some ways, yes! God has provided the perfect place for us to get the power necessary to grow strong and healthy in our relationship with Him. No, it's not a wildflower like the milkweed. It's the Bible.

When we read the wonderful stories and messages that are in the Bible, our faith grows. We shed our selfish skins over and over again. We find Jesus in the Bible. We leave behind our sinful habits, and we become the children God wants us to be. In a world filled with dangerous foods (wrong deeds, selfish thoughts), we have discovered our very own milkweed plant.

Then Jesus said, "I am the bread that gives life. He who comes to me will never be hungry. He who believes in me will never be thirsty" (John 6:35).

The monarch caterpillar needs a special type of food to survive.

The Monarch's Journey 2

Transformation

After enjoying life on the milkweed plant for a couple weeks, something incredible happens. The caterpillar will stop eating the leaves, attach itself to a sturdy part of the plant, bend itself into a "J" shape, and shed its skin one last time. The new covering won't look like a caterpillar anymore. It will have become a chrysalis—a firm structure that starts green and becomes see-through in time.

Safe inside its chrysalis, most of the caterpillar dissolves, leaving behind a liquid blend of soft tissue and random, tiny organ parts. Slowly, that liquid and collection of parts begin to form a new body; a new head; a new mouth; some new legs; and, most surprising of all, a pair of wings!

After ten to fourteen days have passed, the chrysalis splits open and out comes something that doesn't look anything like what it was before. Hanging there on the twig, never to eat solid food again, is a brand-new, beautiful monarch butterfly.

The same Creator God that transforms a bulky caterpillar into a delicate butterfly wants to help change us from sad, angry sinners into happy, helpful friends of Jesus. He can do it.

If anyone belongs to Christ, then he is made new.
The old things have gone; everything is made new!
(2 Corinthians 5:17).

Something amazing happens when the monarch is in its chrysalis stage.

The Monarch's Journey 3

Filled With Power

At long last, it's time for the newly formed monarch to break free of its chrysalis and begin its life as a beautiful butterfly. The chrysalis splits open, and the creature wiggles out and hangs nearby, waiting for something amazing to happen.

Much of the liquid that filled the chrysalis is now inside the body of the butterfly. But the body doesn't need it. Something else does. Its wings! At first those wings hang limp and wrinkled on each side of the body. Slowly, the stored liquid begins to be pumped through those withered wings. They fill out—stretching, expanding, and forming exactly what the butterfly needs in order to survive in its new form.

The sun dries the last of the liquid, and the wings begin to move up and down, testing the air. Then, with a delicate *flap, flap, flap*, the monarch butterfly begins to fly from flower to flower, enjoying the sweet nectar waiting inside each blossom.

What an amazing lesson for us. God wants to fill us with His power so that we can share His love with others. God will always be with us as we share the good news that Jesus has died for us with our friends and neighbors.

"Don't be afraid! Don't worry!
I have always told you what will happen.
You are my witnesses"
(Isaiah 44:8).

The monarch butterfly waits to fill its wings.

The Monarch's Journey 4

The Way Home

Monarch means "someone in charge" or "king" or "queen." We have watched this queen of the sky go from a tiny egg to a lovely creature, flying from flower to flower in a garden or resting beside a pool of water in the woods. But the most surprising thing about this creature is what it does in the fall of the year. It flies home to a place it's never been before.

Millions of monarchs make their way south to Mexico or California where they spend the winter in the very same trees that their parents or grandparents spent their winters. How do they know how to get there? Scientists say it's a mystery, but we know better.

Monarchs are able to fly south to their special trees because God has placed instructions in their tiny minds. He guides them over rugged mountains, through dark forests, across dangerous rivers, or along hot desert valleys. God shows them the way home.

That same God can guide *us* through life and help *us* face whatever dangers get in our way. And like the monarch, our journey will end at a tree too—the tree of life in heaven.

He gives me rest in green pastures.
He leads me to calm water.
He gives me new strength.
For the good of his name,
he leads me on paths that are right (Psalm 23:2, 3).

The beautiful monarch butterfly heads out into the unknown.

Animal Pledge

I pledge to

- stay alert for signs of animal cruelty,
- report animal cruelty to my parents and ask them to report it to law enforcement,
- take care good care of my own pets and ask my friends to do the same,
- ask my parents to sign up to receive important news and alerts from the American Society for the Prevention of Cruelty to Animals.

Animal Journal

Date:

Animal name:

Three important lessons I learned from this animal:

1.

2.

3.

Date:

Animal name:

Three important lessons I learned from this animal:

1.

2.

3.

Date:

Animal name:

Three important lessons I learned from this animal:

1.

2.

3.

Date:

Animal name:

Three important lessons I learned from this animal:

1.

2.

3.

Date:

Animal name:

Three important lessons I learned from this animal:

1.

2.

3.

Date:

Animal name:

Three important lessons I learned from this animal:

1.

2.

3.

Date:

Animal name:

Three important lessons I learned from this animal:

1.

2.

3.

Date:

Animal name:

Three important lessons I learned from this animal:

1.

2.

3.

Start your own Surprising Nature book by drawing or pasting pictures of your favorite critters here.